Poetical
Ikebana

Poetical

stichting kunstboek

two wild ducks
alighting on my pond
a brace forever

Herman Van Rompuy

Introduction

For Westerners, nature is a beautiful and inspirational force, but at the same time it is a powerful and disturbing energy that needs to be curbed and channeled. We try to subordinate nature to human utility and make it a commodity. Our ability to do so manifests our separateness from it. For the Japanese, nature is inevitably linked to existence. True to Buddhist beliefs, man does not stand opposite to nature, but is merely a part of it. Nature and culture belong to the same dimension.

Haiku is a Japanese verse form, originating in the 17th century. It is a simple poem in which it is to see and understand, to detect and comprehend, and to translate an observation in a limited number of lines and sounds or on. Traditionally a haiku comprises of three phrases of respectively 5, 7 and 5 on. Juxtaposition of images is key in haiku. It is the only type of poetry to take nature and the seasons as primary subjects and to use these images of nature as a means to communicate a message, an idea or emotion. Nature speaks through the eyes and words of the poet.

Both Ikebana and haiku are practiced worldwide. Former European President Herman Van Rompuy has brought haiku in the limelight again in Belgium. By making haiku a part of his political and daily life, the almost forgotten and often overlooked art of haiku regained popularity, with an increasing number of haiku-enthusiasts as a result. Haiku learns that even though day-to-day life and reality may look hard, boring and uninteresting at first glance, there is beauty and poetry to be found for those digging a little bit deeper than the surface. In essence, even though it is materialized in another shape, Ikebana wants to convey the same message.

Ikebana and haiku have the power to move people. They evoke emotions using material that has carefully been trimmed of the superfluous. Their minimalism is convincing and reveals the essence. What is left out is just as important as what has been put in. The empty spaces in the arrangements and the unwritten words in haiku play as vital a role as the ones that are there. It takes a discerning eye to distinguish the essential from the superficial and special skill to transform this essence into a concrete shape. Therefore both art disciplines require self-discipline in study and practice.

Working and co-operating closely with nature in making a floral arrangement or a haiku, give a sense of humility and truth. The joy of producing a thing of beauty satisfies the creative urge. Ikebana and haiku are natural tranquillizers. The moment you start to create with nature, the mind is so concentrated that all problems and worldly matters seem to disappear for a moment. You feel relaxed and fulfilled by having created harmony and beauty.

As haiku and ikebana transcend nature by using nature, the two disciplines make for a very successful marriage. Poetical Ikebana wants to emphasize this fruitful interaction. The book shows how traditional and contemporary haiku are interpreted by Ikebana-artists worldwide. And thus how life itself is visualized in a rich diversity of fantastic and inspirational images that stir the senses and touch the heart.

Mit Ingelaere-Brandt

Ikenobo

Ono no Imoko, a priest from the Prince Regent's retinue, decided to retreat from active life after three official journeys to the imperial palace in China. He took charge of the Buddhist temple Rokkaku-do in Kyoto and settled in a little house *ike-no-bo* or *cabin by the lake*. Among the things he had learned in China was the art of offering up flowers at religious ceremonies. He started to study the symbolism and meaning of flowers. This is how the history of Ikebana in Japan began. From then on, many priests devoted themselves to the art of flower arranging. During the second half of the 15th century Senkei XII laid down the first rules of the formal upright rikka style, therefore he is regarded as the founder of the Ikenobo school. Autumn 1629 saw the very first Ikenobo exhibition, an event that is still organized every year. Other styles such as nageira, shoka and moribana developed and imported flowers made their entrance. Traditional values and principles are still respected and held in high esteem, but Ikenobo does open itself for influences of modern times. Every style evolves, but sticks to certain rules. Only freestyle Ikenobo offers endless possibilities for arrangements, ranging from natural to abstract.

Ohara

The Ohara school was founded by Unshin Ohara. After a thorough study of Ikenobo he decided to develop a more personal style: moribana. In moribana the flowers are no longer arranged from a central viewpoint, but are designed in the space of an asymmetric triangle. Unshin designed flat dishes for the new style of arranging and introduced the kenzan, a new flower arranging device. This enabled him to integrate the newly imported flowers in the designs. The moribana style was a true revolution. Although there are many subcategories (colour scheme moribana, landscape moribana, upright style, slanting style, etc), Ohara always puts emphasis on the natural shapes of plants and flowers. Observing nature is of paramount importance, as well as the experience of seasonal difference. Rimpa are colourful and decorative arrangements based on the paintings of Korin, bunjin are spontaneous, artistic arrangements - inspired by the paintings and poetry of the 6th century Chinese aristocracy - in which the expressiveness of the piece is more important than the rules.

Sogetsu

This most recent Ikebana school has the greatest number of members in the world. The school was founded in 1927 by Sofu Teshigahara. At the tender age of seven, he was introduced in the art by his father, who had studied many styles of Ikebana. Sofu soon discovered that Ikebana had more possibilities than the styles that had been practiced until then. Ikebana arrangements had always been displayed in a tokonoma. Sofu saw enormous potential in placing it in every interior. His Sogetsu school believes that anyone can arrange Ikebana anywhere, and with almost anything. Ikebana should be part of a lifestyle to be appreciated by many people, rather than being considered an exclusive art to be enjoyed by few. In the beginning, he cast off all Ikebana rules, but gradually understood how rules were necessary to guide students so that they eventually could be given the freedom of interpretation that is typical of Sogetsu. Just as people are different from each other, Sogetsu encourages Ikebana students to be individual and imaginative.

Ichiyo

The Ichiyo school was founded in 1937 by Meikof Kasuya and his sister Ichiyo. They tried to adapt Ikebana to the modern way of living while retaining traditions, inheritances and rules. In 1983, the third son of Meikof Kasuya; Akihiro, became the third Iemoto of the school. In big stage shows he demonstrated balancing and tension techniques - enabling new and unseen possibilities with flower materials. He urged students to use mainly natural materials and to consider the plant's character, the seasons and the positioning of the arrangement. Ichiyo School encourages personal interpretation. Imagination is considered as essential to creative designs as materials and containers. If flower arranging is to be truly fulfilling, it should be a reflection of oneself.

Jury

Mit Ingelaere-Brandt
Belgium

Mit Ingelaere-Brandt is one of the driving forces behind the flourishing Ikebana scene in Belgium. She took the first grade Sogetsu in 1979. From then on she continued to gain higher grades. Mit teaches Sogetsu, organizes exhibitions and has been involved in sculpting and painting. These fields strongly influence her artistic work. During several years Mit followed courses and masterclasses with Geordie Davidson, she also took several seminars and workshops with Tetsunori Kawana and other Land Art artists such as Helen Escobedo (Mexico) and Bob Verschueren (Belgium). In June 2011 Mit was appointed president of Ikebana International Belgium, a demanding task that made her travel extensively and made her a passionate advocate for the further promotion and development of the noble art of Ikebana. Mit Ingelaere-Brandt has been involved in many of Stichting Kunstboek's publications on Ikebana.

Els Claes
Belgium

Els Claes first discovered Ikenobo and Ikebana when visiting an exhibition of II in Belgium. In 1998 she started her studies under the lead of Lia De Grave-Van Hove (Senior Ikenobo Professor of Ikebana International Belgium). During a first trip to Japan she didn't only travel to see the tourist sites, but also visited the large autumn exhibition at the Ikebana Headquarters. From that moment on, her passion for Ikebana, the Japanese culture and its different art forms only grew stronger. From 2003 onwards, she regularly participated in different seminars in Germany, Switzerland and the Netherlands and contributed to a number of exhibitions. Driven by her enthusiasm to deepen the knowledge of Ikenobo, and encouraged by her professors, she started taking lessons at the Ikenobo Headquarters in Kyoto in 2006. Since then she loves to visit Japan and undertakes a yearly study trip to the Ikenobo Headquarters to continuously broaden her skills and improve her understanding of the art. Professionally Els works as a landscape architect at F-la and is assistant professor.

Godelieve Van den heuvel-Janssens
Belgium

Godelieve Van den heuvel-Janssens originally practiced the traditional styles of the Sesshu Ryu school in Bruges and the Ikenobo style in The Hague, styles that were bound to very strict rules and requirements. During a first study trip to Japan in 1981 she was touched by the natural radiance and freedom of the Ohara School. Godelieve is vice-president and founding member of the Ohara Chapter Belgium and Ikebana International Belgium. She organized and participated in a number of expositions both national and international and frequently gives workshops in Belgium and the Netherlands. Godelieve has been an Ikebana teacher since 1979 (Sesshu) and became Ohara Master in 1990. 2013 saw the publication of Ikebana Ohara. A Song of Flowers, a first retrospective book on her career as Ikebana artist.

Marja Vervoort-Biemond
the Netherlands

Marja is a first grade Sogetsu Ikebana teacher (Somu). From 1975 until 1980, she lived in Taiwan, where brush-painting and Ikebana caught her interest. Back in the Netherlands she passed her exams as a Sogetsu Ikebana teacher. She followed seminars and particpated in workshops in Europe and in the East. Next to several teachers in the Netherlands, she studied with Late Iemoto Hiroshi Teshigahara, Iemoto Akane Teshigahara, Tetsunori Kawana sensei, Eikou Sumura sensei and other master instructors at the headquarters in Tokyo. She aims to create freestyle arrangements and objects with any kind of material in its specific environment. In 2012 Marja had the opportunity to teach Sogetsu classes in Rovaniemi (Finland), in which she used nothing but local materials, found in the arctic circle region. From 2006-2010 she was Branch Director of the Sogetsu Branch Nederland, a function allowed her to share her enthusiasm for Ikebana with other teachers and students all over the world.

Els Goos
the Netherlands

In 1978 Els started taking Sogetsu Ikebana lessons with Rita Uilenreef and after training with Birgit Christensen she obtained her teacher's degree in 1988. To specialize further Els took lessons and workshops with Jeannine Vanhee-Cordeel and Marja Vervoort-Biemond. In Japan she followed a number of courses with Hiroshi and Akane Teshigahara Iemoto and other world-renowned Ikebana teachers such as Shimura, Fukushima, Sumura, Takanaka, Kawana and Nakamura. Els Goos teaches both in the Netherlands and Finland (Rovaniemi) and gave several solo exposition as well as exhibitions together with Sogetsu Branch Nederland, Studiegroep Vlaanderen and Studiegroep Azalea. Els Goos is First Grade Ikebana professor and teaches in Belgium and the Netherlands.

a nightingale
between young bamboo shoots
celebrates the old age

Basho

Mary Marques | Zimbabwe

Birgit Reynders | Belgium

Ursula Winand | Germany

Ohara Study Group Bologna | Italy

Elizabeth Angell | Australia

Rita van der Werf-van den Oudenhoven | the Netherlands

amid the green
one white swan
carried by the blue water

Cecilia Vander Beken

Elizabeth Angell | Australia

Misha Huurman | the Netherlands

Francine Wautelet & Paulette Froidbise | Belgium

Jennie Sterling | USA

Rosemary M.S. Brown | Jersey, Channel Islands (UK)

there comes a butterfly
and with the butterfly from my garden
he flutters away

Issa

Elena Kilchevskaya | Russia

Renate Haskert-Riechel | Germany

Désirée van Vliet | the Netherlands

Ayako Graefe | Gemany

Godelieve Van den heuvel-Janssens | Belgium

Chinara Munduzbaeva | Russia

a summer breeze
suddenly around the corner
caressing our face

Rosa Ternest

Tatiana Tsoy | Russia

Christopher James | Australia

Ilse Neumayer | Austria

looking up proudly
at the old town – bowing deeply
beneath low bridges

Rosa Ternest

Greet Snoodijk | the Netherlands

Elke Jacob | Germany

Hedwigis M. Bogaert-Waterblee | Belgium

Helen Novic | Australia

a cold down-pour -
are pebbles falling now
in the brook full of gravel?

Basho

Esther Hoogland | the Netherlands

Jeroen Th. Vermaas | the Netherlands

Rosemary M.S. Brown | Jersey, Channel Islands (UK) C

still the red sun
is glowing pitiless
but the autumn wind rustles

Basho

Mieke Bruynooghe-Van Elslande | Belgium

Fatima Hanke | Germany

Ingrid Tosei Maier Galvagni | Italy **Wafu Kai**

Brigitta Buse | Germany

Ivy Le Maguer | France

Thérèse Van Overstyns | Belgium

Nelly Cautereels | Belgium

Els Goos | the Netherlands

Van Nguyen | Switzerland

Susan Cano | USA

Olga Yudina | Russia

Denise Adriaensen | Belgium

Betty Karanikolopoulos | Australia

beyond the river
windows reflect the sunshine
water bathes in light

Nadine Victor

Betty Karanikolopoulos | Australia

Siska Van De Steene | Belgium

Ursula Wehr | Germany

Waltraud Zajac | Germany

a grebe passes by
proud like a king on his horse
soon his love dance

Nadine Victor

Hedwigis M. Bogaert-Waterblee | Belgium

raindrops
roll to each other
on the lotus leaf

Shiki

Florence Van Crombrugge-Chaubert | Belgium

where are you now?
in the silence of the room
the echo of an answer

Gilberte Neyt

Joan Norbury | Australia

Monique van de Ven | the Netherlands

Helen Novic | Australia

Elizabeth Lanier Campbell | USA

wild poppy
flame with ashes in the heart
so red, so black

Gilberte Neyt

Lucy Papas | Australia

Annie De Sutter | Belgium

clouds breaking
there in the clear moonlight
the Fuji no Yama

Basho

Hedwigis M. Bogaert-Waterblee | Belgium

Angelika Raatz | Germany

Ivy Le Maguer | France

Els Claes | Belgium

and still, and still again
I bend for the other side
at the end of the year

Issa

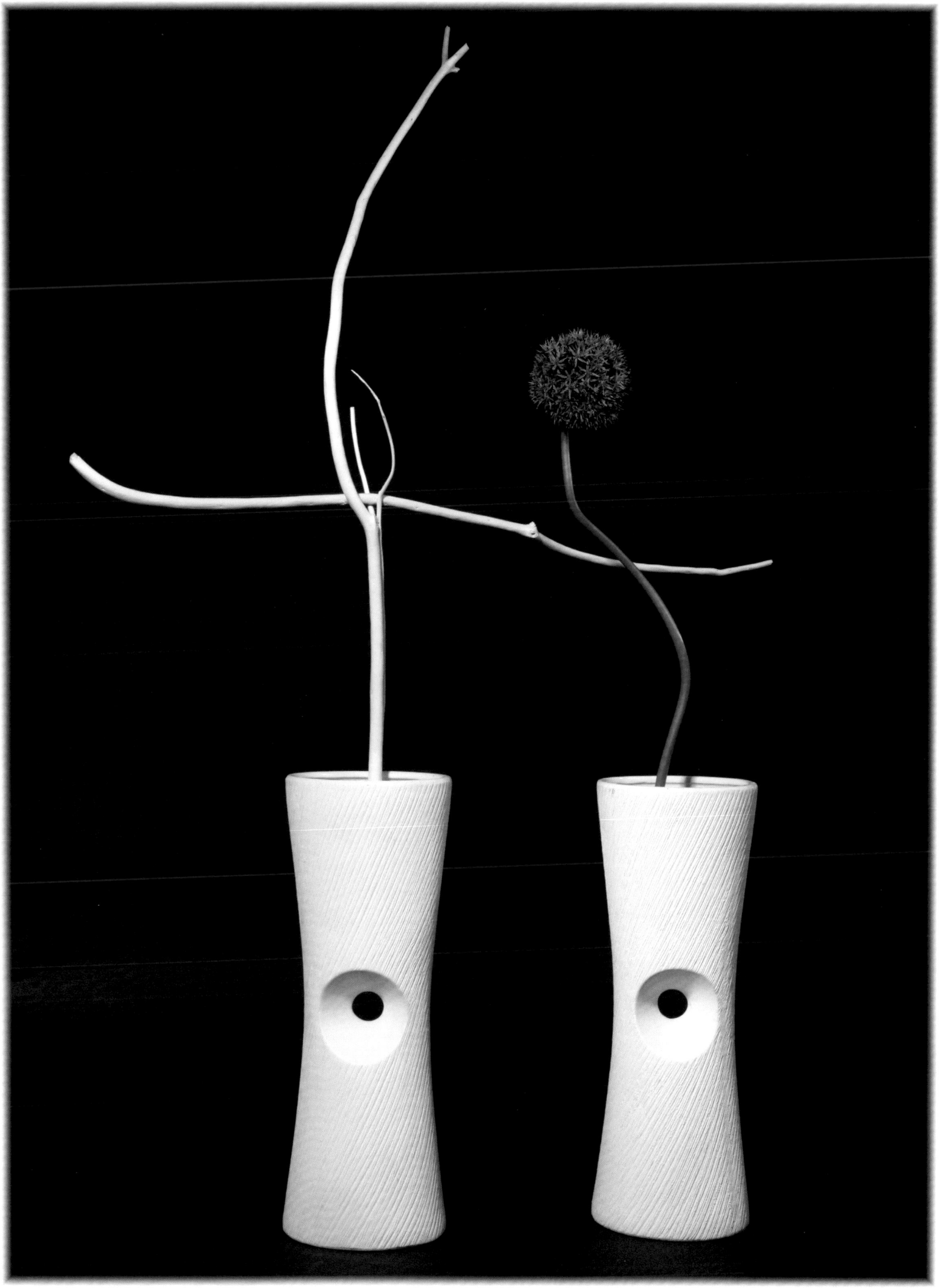

Gabi Krieg | Germany

Helen Novic | Australia

Gerda Matthees | Belgium

Robyn Unglik | Australia

Margaret Wilson | Australia

Mieke Bruynooghe-Van Elslande | Belgium

Wil Oortman | the Netherlands

cold winternight
a starry sky, widely stretched
like a baldachin

Brigitte Staggl

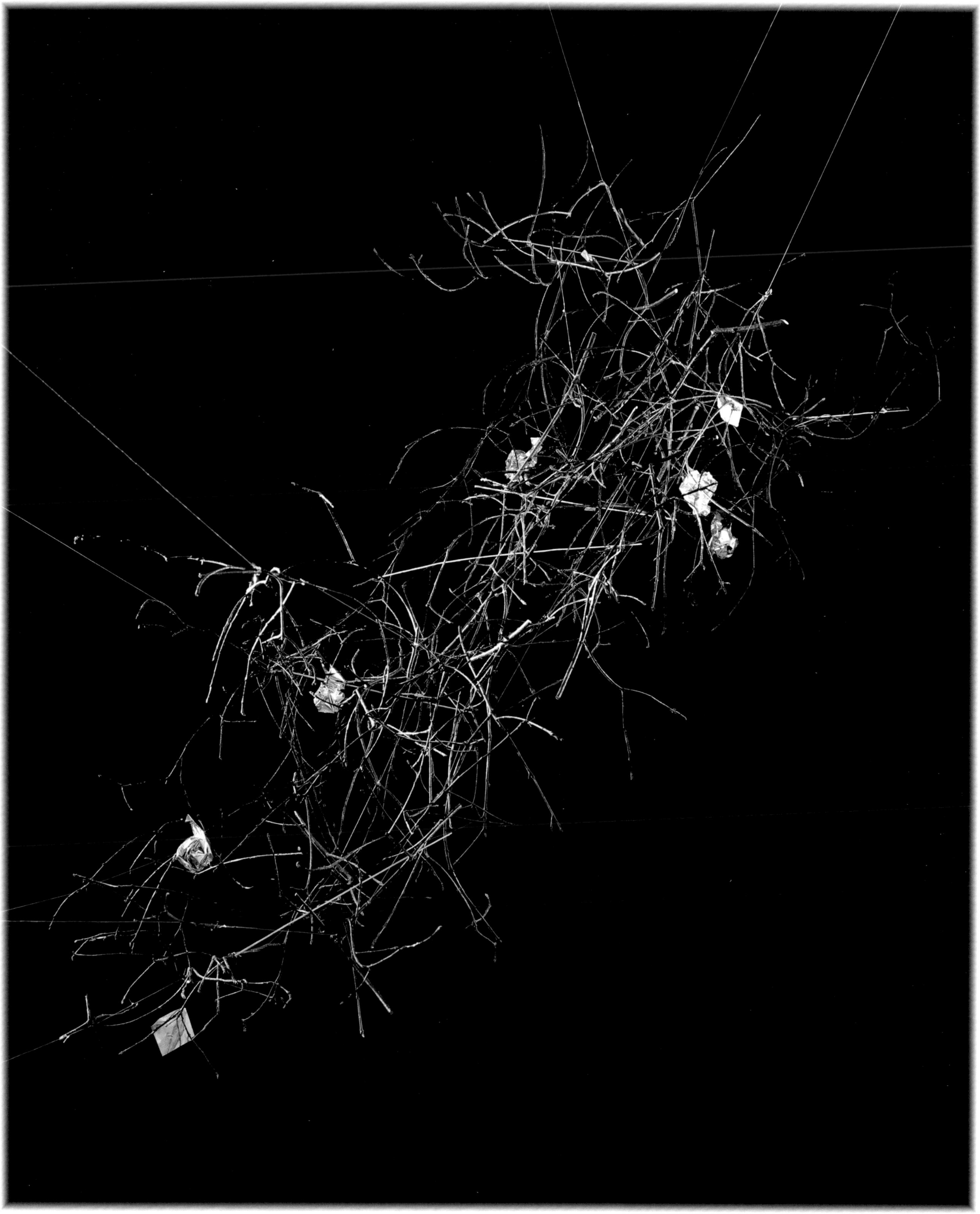

Gulshakhar Suraubaeva | Russia

Anke Verhoeven | the Netherlands

first snow
how quiet do the white flakes
whirl downwards

Brigitte Staggl

Helen M. Hickman | Jersey, Channel Islands (UK) ☾

Urana Kuular | Russia

Neonila Yefimova | Ukraine

Els Goos | the Netherlands

red poppies,
when the mist clears away
they already move

Shiro

Els Goos | the Netherlands

Els Goos | the Netherlands

heavy winter storm –
above the sea stars
are blown into the water

Shiki

Chinara Munduzbaeva | Russia

Dominique Coudroy / Groupe Le Teich | France

Els Claes | Belgium

still the earth wears
its dress of summer days
covered in gold leaf

Monika Burghoff

Georgine du Quesne van Bruchem-Meiners | France

Godelieve Van den heuvel-Janssens | Belgium

Randa Muammar Kawar | Jordan

he doesn’t loosen
although shaken up by the wind
– the last apple

Monika Burghoff

Marja Vervoort-Biemond | the Netherlands

Birgit Reynders | Belgium

Robyn Unglik | Australia

the shore and the boat
talk to each other
for the day's so long

Shiki

Robyn Unglik | Australia

Mary Pearson | Northern Ireland (UK)

Emily Karanikolopoulos | Australia

Rumiko Manako | Japan

Rita Dollberg | Germany

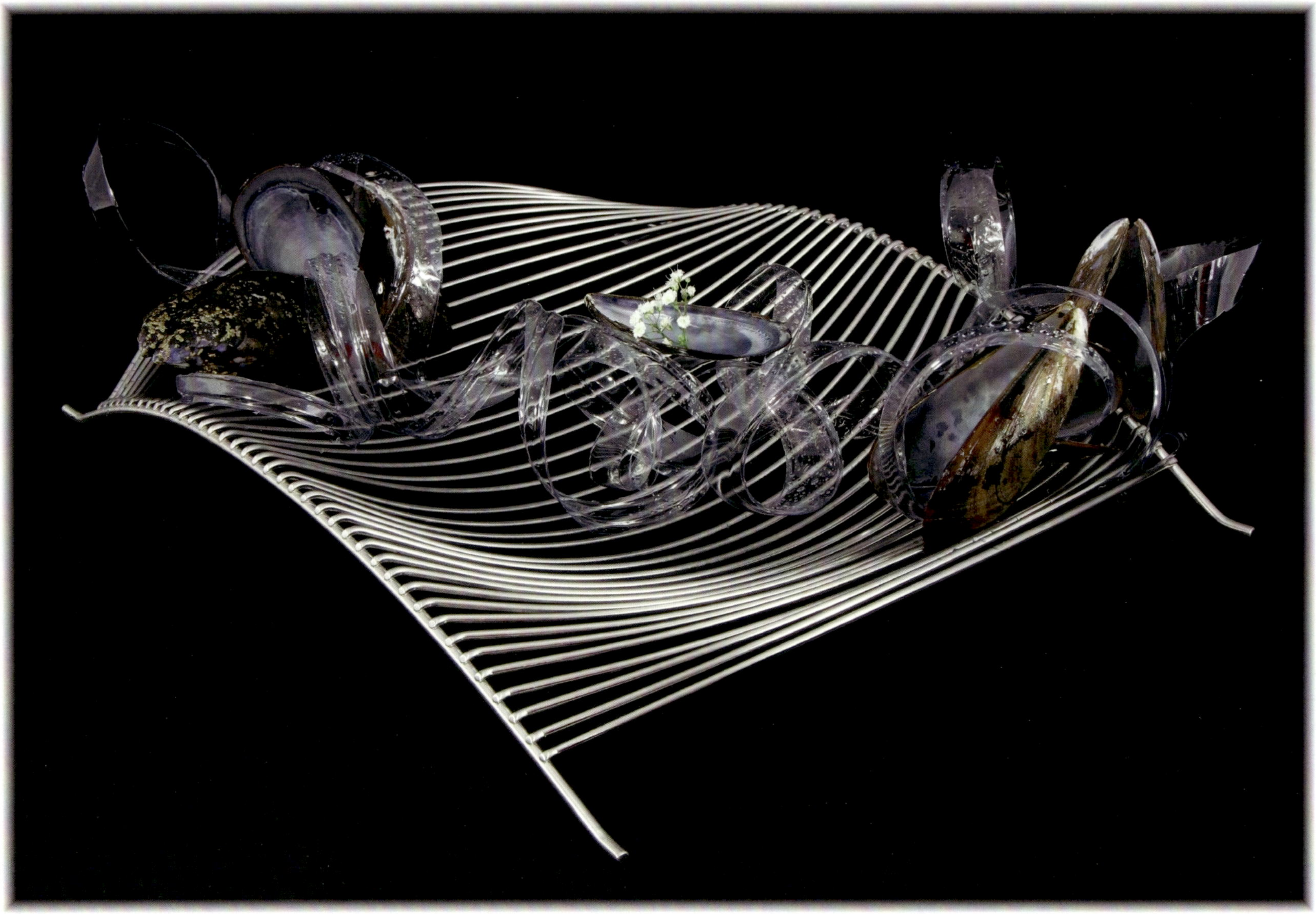

Elin Dahlin | Sweden

Gulshakhar Suraubaeva | Russia

the spring is fading
it hesitates for a long time
in the late blossoms

Buson

Claire Delort | France

Marcel Vrignaud | France

just before dawn
the whole universe filled
by one blackbird

Ann Colpaert

Emily Karanikolopoulos | Australia

Betty Karanikolopoulos | Australia

Marta Lanfranco | Italy **Wafu Kai**

only the barking
let me hear the silence -
a dark night

Ann Colpaert

Doriana Bonafede | Italy **Wafu Kai**

Karoline Van Bever | Belgium

my garden in the sun
there two white butterflies
plait garlands

Hedwig Aerts

Gulshakhar Suraubaeva | Russia

Susan Cano | USA

Theresa Feile | Australia

Riita Hurme | Finland

I had forgotten
that children coloured
the streets so brightly

Hedwig Aerts

Denise Adriaensen | Belgium

without any noise
the peony falls to pieces
in the middle of the night

Shiki

Chinara Munduzbaeva | Russia

Larisa Sarycheva | Russia

black, tender and proud
the heron overlooks
the peaceful ocean

Andrea Van den Haute

Hedwigis M. Bogaert-Waterblee | Belgium

Mieke Bruynooghe-Van Elslande | Belgium

cherry blossoms whirl
in the water of the ricefield –
night of moon and stars

Buson

Elke Jacob | Germany C

a lightning flash –
the sound of water drops
falling through bamboo

Buson

Ursula Winand | Germany

Margaret Wilson | Australia

Christophe Capdeville | France

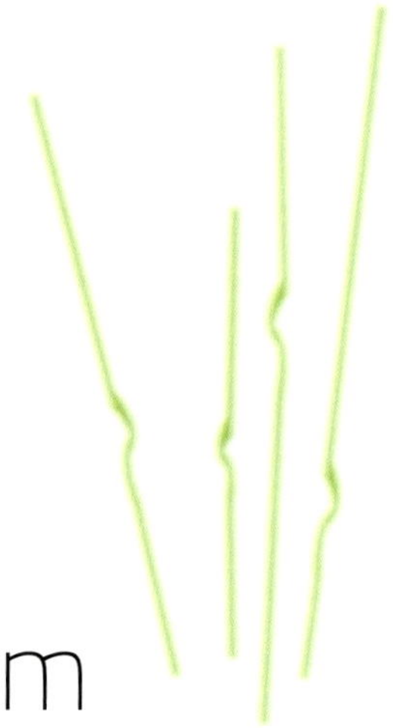

the winter storm
hid in the bamboo grove
and quieted away

Basho

Roswitha Kluge | Germany

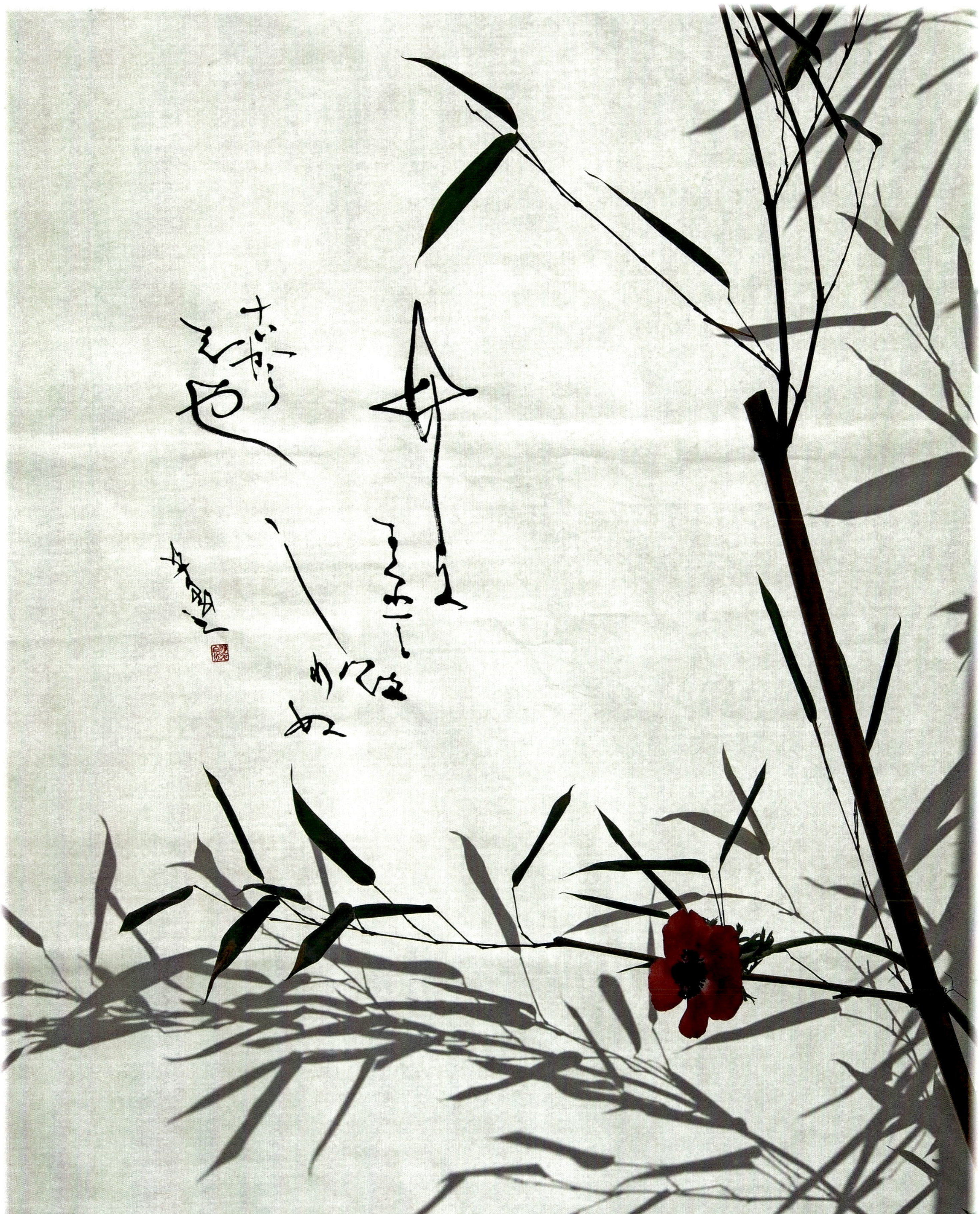

Antje Klatt | Germany

a clear waterfall -
into the ripples
fall green pine-needles

Basho

Sandra Marker | Australia

Dominique Coudroy / Groupe Le Teich | France

Theresa Feile | Australia

Susan Cano | USA

Waltraud Zajac | Germany

Participants

Denise Adriaensen
Belgium **Sogetsu | Ohara**
Photography: Lieve Janssens
- p 68: Cornus sericea, Hippeastrum 'Sydney', Salix babylonica
- p 78-79: Choisya 'Aztec Pearl', Hippeastrum 'Clown', Phoenix dactylifera
- p 168: Mitsumata, Protea

Elizabeth Angell
Australia **Sogetsu**
Photography: Nick Dale
- p 16: Celosia cristata, bamboo (black)
- p 19: Amaryllis, Doryanthes excelsa (leaves), Lavandula

Rica Arai
France **Sogetsu**
Photography: Yosuke Kojima
- p 155: Prunus
- p 196: Pinus

Ilse Beunen
Belgium **Sogetsu**
Photography: Ben Huybrechts
- p 23: Equisetum hyemale, Phalaenopsis

Hedwigis Bogaert-Waterblee
Belgium **Sogetsu**
Photography: Foto Daniel
- p 41: Aspidistra elatior, Cactus cereus, Malus sylvestris var. domestica, Skimma japonica
- p 77: Anthurium, Aspidistra elatior, Vitis vinifera
- p 97: Platicerium, driftwood
- p 177: Aspidistra elatior, Juncus, glass

Doriana Bonafede
Italy **Wafu Kai**
Photography: Nicola Galvagni
Portrait: Piero Enrione
- p 158: Cymbidium leaves, Zantedeschia aethiopica

Adriaan Braamse
the Netherlands **Sogetsu**
Photography: Désirée van Vliet
- p 182-183: Alstroemeria, Anemone

Jean Brouwers
the Netherlands **Sogetsu**
Photography: Désirée van Vliet
- p 85: Anthurium, Nelumbo nucifera (leaf)
- p 149: Anthurium (leaf), Hamamelis, Zantedeschia

Rosemary M.S. Brown
United Kingdom **Sogetsu**
Photography: Steve Wellum
- p 25: Cytisus, Helleborus, Strelitzia leaf (dry)
- p 48: Camellia, Forsythia intermedia

Mieke Bruynooghe-Van Elslande
Belgium **Sogetsu**
Photography: Kate Neels
Portrait: D. Bruynooghe
- p 51: Capsicum, Xerophyllum tenax
- p 108: Aspidistra leaf (dry), Xerophyllum tenax
- p 178: Hypericum, Xerophyllum tenax

Brigitta Buse
Germany **Sogetsu**
Photography: Felix Buse
- p 60: Agave ferox, Heliconia rostrata

Elizabeth Lanier Campbell
USA **Ichiyo**
Photography: Julie McMillan
- p 45: Phormium, Xerophyllum tenax, Hamamelis
- p 82: Nelumbo nucifera
- p 90: Hosta fortunei, Liriope, Paeonia suffruticosa

Susan Cano
USA **Sogetsu**
Photography: Patti Quinn Hill
- p 66: Dianthus caryophyllus, Miscanthus sinensis, bamboo
- p 162: Gypsophila 'Million Stars', Phalaenopsis, Salix discolor
- p 200: Pinus mugo, Salix caprea pendula

Christophe Capdeville
France **Ichiyo**
Photography: Christophe Capdeville
- p 188: Anemone, Chaenomeles japonica, Viburnum tinus

Nelly Cautereels
Belgium **Ohara**
Photography: Jef Cuylen
- p 63: Akebia quinata, Tulipa

Natalia Cherkashina
Russia **Sogetsu**
Photography: Yulia Mikityak
- p 95: Anemone, Calamus rotang, Xerophyllum tenax

Eugenia Chudacek
Australia **Sogetsu**
Photography: Eugenia Chudacek
Portrait: Clare Chudacek
- p 56: Pinus radiata

Els Claes
Belgium **Ikenobo**
Photography: Els Claes
- p 101: Anthurium, Camassia leichtlinii 'Caerulea', Craspedia globosa, Eucalyptus pulverulenta, Gypsophila
- p 113: Azalea, Dracaena fragrans 'Compacta', Eryngium alpinum, Eucalyptus pulverulenta, Hyacinthoides, Leucadendron, Spiraea thunbergii
- p 127: Brunnera macrophylla 'Hadspen Cream', Camassia leichtlinii 'Caerulea', Xanthoriza simplicissima

Dominique Coudroy / Groupe Le Teich
France **Sogetsu**
Members: Josy Nougé, Andrée Daycard, Marie Dallot, Yoko Lartigue, Dominique Coudroy
Photography: Marie Dallot
- p 126: Primula vulgaris, Salix babylonica
- p 197: Begonia sp., Pinus pinaster

Elin Dahlin
Sweden **Sogetsu**
Photography: Elin Dahlin
Portrait: Miguel Lopez Velasco
- p 144: Gypsophila, Mytilus edulis, plastic

Annie De Sutter
Belgium **Ikenobo**
Photography: Yen De Spiegelaere
Portrait: Toos Vergote
- p 94: Lycopodium clavatum, Papaver nudicaule, Xanthorrhoea preissii

Claire Delort
France **Ikenobo**
Photography: Fabien Bernardi
Portrait: Olivier Delort
- p 147: Camellia, Codiaeum, Dianthus barbatus 'Green Trick', Hypericum, Lathytus odoratus, Lilicophyta, Paeonia, Panicum virgatum, Salix matsudana, Solidago, Veronica, Zantedeschia

Rita Dollberg
Germany **Sogetsu**
Photography: P.G. Loske
- p 143: Sarracenia, Primula

Georgine du Quesne van Bruchem-Meiners
France **Ichiyo**
Photography: N. du Quesne van Bruchem
- p 130: Alstroemeria ligtu, Ficus carica, Ginkgo biloba, Rosa

Nabiha El Kefi
United Arab Emirates **Sogetsu**
Photography: L. Kefi
- p 157: Bougainvillea spectabilis, Sansevieria trifasciata, bleached branches

Ohara Study Group Bologna
Italy **Ohara**
Members: MP. Tarquinii, E. Galli, F. De Leo, E. Galassi, G. Sabbi, E. Arsani, E. Gatti, L. Maserati, F. Quareni, L. Linari, G. Stupazzini
Photography: Margherita Cecchini, Beatrice Marchi
- p 14: Camellia japonica, Lilium longiflorum, Philodendron selloum, bamboo
- p 15: Ranunculus, Strelitzia, bamboo, bamboo roots

Huda Fallaha
Jordan **Sogetsu**
Photography: George H. Lepedjian
- p 189: Gypsophila 'Million Stars', Heliconia bihai 'Giant Lobster Claw', Sinarundinaria murielae

Theresa Feile
Australia **Sogetsu**
Photography: Nick Dale
- p 164: Ligustrum, Malus germanica, Rosae
- p 198: Pinus, rocks, water

Angelika Gorlitz
Germany **Sogetsu**
Photography: Wolfgang Raatz
Portrait: Angelika Raatz
- p 31: Cornus, Hypericum, Ornithogalum

Els Goos
the Netherlands **Sogetsu**
Photography: Els Goos
- p 64: Euonymus, Euphorbia, Gerbera, Hosta
- p 119: Gypsophila, Salix, Zantedeschia
- p 122: Cryptomeria, Gypsophila, Papaver
- p 123: Gypsophila, Papaver

Ayako Graefe
Germany **Sogetsu**
Photography: Volker Graefe
Portrait: Helmuth E. Günther
- p 30: Asparagus plumosus, Phalaenopsis, bamboo

Minh Haeusler
Switzerland **Sogetsu**
Photography: Minh Haeusler
Portrait: Thomas Haeusler
- p 129: Physalis alkekengi

Participants

Fatima Hanke
Germany **Sogetsu**
Photography: Wolfgang Raatz
Portrait: Angelika Raatz
- p 54: Strelitzia, cardboard

Misha Huurman
the Netherlands **Sogetsu**
Photography: Désirée van Vliet
- p 20: Gentiana, Strelitzia, bleached palm leaf
- p 43: Anthurium, Anthurium leaf

Toula-Dimitra Karanikolopoulos
Australia **Sogetsu**
Photography: Nick Dale
- p 21: Cucurbita pepo, Lilium

Renate Haskert-Riechel
Germany **Sogetsu**
Photography: Wolfgang Raatz
Portrait: Angelika Raatz
- p 28: Phalaenopsis, Typha, paper

Mit Ingelaere-Brandt
Belgium **Sogetsu**
Photography: Annika Ingelaere
- p 4: Anthurium, Aspidistra, Iris leaves
- p 163: Camellia, Magnolia

Philip T. Keon
Australia **Sogetsu**
Photography: Fiona Hamilton
- p 117: Gypsophila

Edelgard Herwald
Germany **Sogetsu**
Photography: Barry Alsop
- p 131: Jacaranda cuspidifolia, Lechenaultia divaricata (tumbleweed

Elke Jacob
Germany **Sogetsu**
Photography: Elke Jacob
Portrait: Anja Fengler
- p 40: Equisetum, Papaveraceae
- p 181: Anthurium creantum (leaves), Rosa 'George Burns'

Elena Kilchevskaya
Russia **Sogetsu**
Photography: Alexei Popov
- p 27: Gloriosa, Chamelaucium, Muscus, Picea
- p 170: Clematis, Lily grass

Helen M. Hickman
United Kingdom **Sogetsu**
Photography: Steve Wellum
- p 115: Chamelaucium uncinatum, Prunus cerasifera

Christopher James
Australia **Sogetsu**
Photography: Christopher James
Portrait: NALU Productions
- p 36: Pinus radiata

Antje Klatt
Germany **Sogetsu**
Photography: Antje Klatt
Portrait: Karin Offinger
- p 193: Anemone coronaria, Phyllostachys aureosilcata 'Spectabilis'

Esther Hoogland
the Netherlands **Sogetsu**
Photography: Frank Kho
- p 46: Eucalyptus (leaves), Muscari, Salix babylonica
- p 83: Cordyline negro, Phalaenopsis

Betty Karanikolopoulos
Australia **Sogetsu**
Photography: Nick Dale
- p 69: Doryanthes excelsa, Helianthus, wood, steel
- p 71: glass container, water, wood frames
- p 153: Sago palm leaves, Strelitzia nicolai

Roswitha Kluge
Germany **Ikenobo**
Photography: Renate & Mathias Tautermann
- p 192: Gypsophila, Lilium, Pseudosasa japonica

Riita Hurme
Finland **Sogetsu**
Photography: Kalevi Hujanen
Portrait: Tiina Viitala/VIVA Images Finland Oy
- p 165: Anthurium andreanum, metal netting, glass container

Emily Karanikolopoulos
Australia **Sogetsu**
Photography: Nick Dale
- p 141: Carex trifida (variegated leaves), Geranium (variegated leaves), Hydrangea macrophylla, Picea pungens (dwarf)
- p 152: Iris japonica (variegated leaves), Iris spuria (leaves), Strelitzia nicolai, tumble weed (dried)

Gabi Krieg
Germany **Sogetsu**
Photography: Pamela Schulze
- p 103: Allium giganteum, Edgeworthia chrysantha

Nicole Kruimel-Rosselle
the Netherlands **Sogetsu**
Photography: Bram Kruimel
Portrait: Bas Vernooij
- p 57: Agave, electric wire

Mary Marques
Zimbabwe **Sogetsu**
Photography: Leah Nachipo
Portrait: Linda Marques
- p 11: Bambusa vulgaris, Phalaenopsis

Joan Norbury
Australia **Sogetsu**
Photography: Joan Norbury
Portrait: Lois Thompson
- p 87: Begonia coccinea (cane-stemmed Begonia)
- p 151: Eucalyptus camaldulensis (weathered wood)

Urana Kuular
Russia **Sogetsu**
Photography: Urana Kuular
- p 116: Bouvardia 'Diamond White', Gleichenia, Trachelium 'Lake Powell'

Gerda Matthees
Belgium **Sogetsu**
Photography: Guy Dierckens
- p 105: Rhopalostylis sapida, Skimmia
- p 191: Ginkgo biloba, bamboo

Helen Novic
Australia **Sogetsu**
Photography: Nick Dale
- p 42: Epidendrum, Opuntia coccinellifera, timber offcut, rusted metal
- p 89: Hydrangea macrophylla, metal, glass plate
- p 104: Celosia argentea var. cristata, dried branch

Marta Lanfranco
Italy **Wafu Kai**
Photography: Nicola Galvagni
Portrait: Luca Simoncella
- p 154: Gypsophila paniculata, Limonium, Rhapis humilis, Zantedeschia pentlandii

Randa Muammar Kawar
Jordan **Sogetsu**
Photography: Fakhri Al-Alami
- p 133: Euonymus japonica, Limonium, Strelitzia (dry leaves)

Liisa Nurminen, Jyrki Setala, Aino Ruutu
Finland **Sogetsu**
Photography: Yurki Setälä
- p 98: Chrysanthemum santini, Gypsophila, Leucospermum, Livistonia chinensis, Pinus, split bamboo

Ivy Le Maguer
France **Ikenobo**
Photography: Armelle Corre
Portrait: Guylaine Sery-Stazzu
- p 61: Camellia japonica, Sasa veitchii, lichened wood
- p 100: Camellia japonica, Ceanothus thyrsiflorus, Chamaecyparis obtusa, Eriobotrya japonica (loquat), Forsythia, Iris hollandica, Pinus, Pseudosasa japonica

Chinara Munduzbaeva
Russia **Sogetsu**
Photography: Alexey Popov
- p 33: Anemone, Camellia, Livingstonia (bleached), Xanthorrhoea
- p 125: Amaryllis, split bamboo
- p 173: Liriope, Paeonia

Rumiko Manako
Japan **Ikenobo**
Photography: Rumiko Manako
- p 142: Iris laevigata

Ilse Neumayer
Austria **Sogetsu**
Photography: Bernhard Neumayer
- p 37: Panicum virgatum, Rosa
- p 59: Forsythia (leaves), Rosa canina

Wil Oortman
the Netherlands **Sogetsu**
Photography: Moniek van de Ven
- p 109: Hippeastrum (yellow), Hydrangea (branch), Picea conica

Sandra Marker
Australia **Sogetsu**
Photography: Sandra Marker
Portrait: Doug Marker
- p 195: Euphorbia milii, Pinus radiata

Van Nguyen
Switzerland **Ikenobo**
Photography: Van Nguyen
- p 65: Anthurium leaf, Curculigo, Gloriosa, Heliconia, Vanda

Lucy Papas
Australia **Sogetsu**
Photography: Nick Dale
- p 93: Salix babylonica (spraypainted stripped branches), Watsonia

Participants

Mary Pearson
Northern Ireland (UK) **Sogetsu**
Photography: Stephen Pearson
- p 140: Anthurium andreanum, Phormium tenax

Denise Priem-Willemarck
Belgium **Sogetsu**
Photography: Denise Priem-Willemarck
- p 55: Calamus rotang, Pinus, Rosa

Angelika Raatz
Germany **Sogetsu**
Photography: Wolfgang Raatz
- p 99: Alocasia sanderiana, Jatropha podagrica

Birgit Reynders
Belgium **Sogetsu**
Photography: Ben Huybrechts
- p 12: Fargesia nitida, Phyllostachys aureosilcata 'Aureocaulis', Tulipa
- p 136: Fagus, paper

Lea Ruprecht
Switzerland **Sogetsu**
Photography: Lea Ruprecht
Portrait: Jörg Ruprecht
- p 72: Helianthus annuus, Xanthorrhoea

Larisa Sarycheva
Russia **Sogetsu**
Photography: Eleonora Drykina
- p 171: Equisetum, Strelitzia, coloured pencils
- p 174: Paeonia, coloured water

Henriette Schalk
the Netherlands **Sogetsu**
Photography: Henriette Schalk
- p 49: Amelanchier (stem), Viburnum x bodnantense 'Charles Lamont'
- p 167: Calamus rotang (green), Hyancinthus flowers

Ekaterina Seehaus
Belgium **Sogetsu**
Photography: Frank Van den Block
Portrait: Martin Seehaus
- p 169: Gerbera, Phragmites
- p 185: Alstroemeria, Salix, bamboo

Greet Snoodijk
the Netherlands **Sogetsu**
Photography: Frank Kho
- p 39: Anemone, Limonium, bleached twigs

Jennie Sterling
USA **Sogetsu**
Photography: Terence Warwick
- p 24: Cyperus altenifolius, Cyperus papyrus 'Nana', Chondropetalum tectorum, Daucus carota (Ammi), Juncus effusus, Lilium, Philodendron 'Xanadu'

Gulshakhar Suraubaeva
Russia **Sogetsu**
Photography: Alexey Popov
- p 111: Alnus, wooden sticks, metallized scotch tape
- p 145: Betula (wood), Spathiphyllum, mirror
- p 161: Fritillaria alba, Gypsophila, Phalaenopsis, Schoenus melanostachys

Larisa Telford
Autralia **Sogetsu**
Photography: Vladimir Tsyskin
- p 81: Nelumbo nucifera (leaves and flowers)

Ingrid Tosei Maier Galvagni
Italy **Wafu Kai**
Photography: Nicola Galvagni
Portrait: Alessio Ferrarese
- p 58: Dianthus caryophyllus, Miscanthus sinensis (Suzuki grass)

Tatiana Tsoy
Russia **Sogetsu**
Photography: Alexey Popov
- p 35: Alstroemeria, Chrysanthemum santini, Xerophyllum tenax, mitsumata

Robyn Unglik
Australia **Sogetsu**
Photography: Nick Dale
- p 106: Agapanthus africanus, steel strapping
- cover, p 137: Malus domestica, steel strapping
- p139: Epidendrum, Hennedya crispa (seaweed), lichenes

Karoline Van Bever
Belgium **Sogetsu**
Photography: Annika Ingelaere
- p 159: Cornus, Iris, driftwood

Florence Van Crombrugge-Chaubert
Belgium **Sogetsu**
Photography: Michel Desmet
- p 84: Nelumbo nucifera (dried leaves and seedpods)

Siska Van De Steene
Belgium **Sogetsu**
Photography: Annika Ingelaere
- p 73: Lilium

Monique van de Ven
the Netherlands **Sogetsu**
Photography: Erik Teubner
Portrait: Monique van de Ven
- p 88: Aronia melanocarpa, Helianthus annuus, Ligustrum

Jeroen Th. Vermaas
the Netherlands **Ichiyo**
Photography: Jeroen Vermaas
Portrait: Willemijn Vermaas
- p 47: Lonicera peryclimenum, Xanthorrhoea preissii, Ranunculus
- p 91: Clematis x jackmannii, Salix alba 'Tristis'

Ursula Winand
Germany **Sogetsu | Ikenobo**
Photography: Werner Möhler
- p 2-3: Anthurium, Bromelioideae, Palmae, driftwood
- p 13: Bambusoideae, Medinilla magnifica
- p 186: Bambusoideae, Poncirus trifoliata, Zingiber officinale (flower)

Godelieve Van den heuvel-Janssens
Belgium **Ohara**
Photography:
Portrait and p 132: Peter Staes
p 32: Lieve Janssens
- p 32: Nandina domestica, Camellia
- p 132: Cotoneaster horizontalis, Helianthus annuus, Heuchera

Marja Vervoort-Biemond
the Netherlands **Sogetsu**
Photography: Els Goos
- p 135: Anemone bleached, wood

Mitzi Yau
Canada **Ohara**
Photography: Helen Chu
- p 175: Paeonia lactiflora pall., Camellia japonica, Magnolia L.

Rita van der Werf-van den Oudenhoven
the Netherlands **Sogetsu**
Photography: Julia Op den Brouw
- p 17: Catalpa (seed pods), Phalaenopsis, Tulipa (French tulip)

Marcel Vrignaud
France **Ohara**
Photography: Marcel Vrignaud
- p 148: Aesculus hippocastanum, Cryptomeria, Hemerocallis, Narcissus

Neonila Yefimova
Ukraine **Sogetsu**
Photography: Armina Kagramanova
- p 118: Salix, Lilium
- p 179: Zantedeschia, dry palm leaf

Thérèse Van Overstyns
Belgium **Ohara**
Photography: Ch. Van Overstyns
- p 62: Gerbera, Magnolia leaf, Prunus domestica

Francine Wautelet & Paulette Froidbise
Belgium **Sogetsu**
Photography: Annika Ingelaere
- p 22: Glycine, Hydrangea, Spirea, Zantedeschia

Olga Yudina
Russia **Sogetsu**
Photography: Alexey Popov
- p 67: Gleditsia triacanthos, Heliconia
- p 199: Cacti (dried), Muscari armeniacum, Pinus

Désirée van Vliet
the Netherlands **Sogetsu**
Photography: Désirée van Vliet
- p 29: Anthurium (leaf), Tulipa
- p 52: Nelumbo nucifera (dry), Gerbera, bamboo (black)

Ursula Wehr
Germany **Sogetsu**
Photography: Wolfgang Raatz
Portrait: Angelika Raatz
- p 74: Prunus (blossoms), Vanda
- p 121: Prunus (blossoms), Papaver

Waltraud Zajac
Germany **Sogetsu**
Photography: Wolfgang Raatz
Portrait: Angelika Raatz
- p 75: Asparagus plumosus, Begonia, Hydrangea
- p 201: Pinus mugo, Vriesea splendens, Helleborus niger, Raku container

Anke Verhoeven
the Netherlands **Sogetsu**
Photography: Désirée van Vliet
- p 53: Calamus rotang, Gerbera
- p 112: Gypsophila, felt

Margaret Wilson
Australia **Sogetsu**
Photography: Nick Dale
- p 107: Doryanthes excelsa, Ulmus parvifolia
- p 187: Bambusa oldhamii, Strelitzia reginae (dried and painted)

Author
Mit Ingelaere-Brandt

Advisory panel
Els Claes
Els Goos
Mit Ingelaere-Brandt
Godelieve Van den heuvel-Janssens
Marja Vervoort-Biemond

Haiku
Poëziecentrum Gent
Special thanks to Hedwig Aerts, Cecilia Vander Beken, Rosa Ternest, Nadine Victor, Gilberte Neyt, Brigitte Staggl, Monika Burghoff, Andrea Van den Haute and Ann Colpaert for the contemporary haiku.

Final editing
Katrien Van Moerbeke

Lay-out
www.groupvandamme.eu

Print
www.pureprint.be

Published by
Stichting Kunstboek bvba
Legeweg 165
B-8020 Oostkamp
Belgium
Tel. +32 50 46 19 10
Fax. +32 50 46 19 18
info@stichtingkunstboek.com
www.stichtingkunstboek.com

ISBN 978-90-5856-519-8
D/2015/6407/14
NUR 421